———PRAISE FOR———

BATTLE CRY

"*Battle Cry* is a triumph. It is a celebration of survival. May's exquisite use of language describes a life in which all feelings are felt and all experiences are valued. Every moment is prized as a life-building block, especially the anguished. Her book sheds light on the violence many face in the world each day. We need that light. If you doubt that pain and suffering have value, then read this book and be affirmed."

—Susan W. Trestrail, M.A.,M.S.Ed.
Adjunct English Professor

"In *Battle Cry*, Jen May gathers words from the terrible wreckage of a life, and uses them to illuminate the dark wars that underlie too many supposed loves. Consistently powerful and true, her forty-two poems will simultaneously break your heart and teach you much of the courage needed to escape the unexpected enemy."

—Lennart Lundh
So Careless of Themselves

"Jen May writes with a powerful presence—a warrior for sure. Her words touch and mold the heart and rend the reader, seared, towards a haven of sound. She strikes a chord and reminds the reader that they are entitled to an honest experience and rendering of a life well-lived and fought for."

—Heather Lake
Ramblings of an Earnest Mind

Battle Cry

poems by
Jen May

Copyright 2016 © Jen May

All rights reserved.

Cover design by Adam Nicolai
Published by Empty-Grave Publishing

ISBN: 1-62089-017-8
ISBN-13: 978-1-62089-017-2

To those who lift the fallen.

CONTENTS

A BEGINNING: 9

    SUNSET STORY : 11

    UNTITLED : 12

    DANCE OF ASHES : 15

    HOT SPELL : 17

TRIGGER WARNING: BLOOD AND BONE : 19

    UNTITLED : 21

    TERROR TODAY : 22

    INDEPENDENCE DAY : 24

    CURVING AWAY : 26

    SHOCK AND AWE : 28

    FOR NEXT TIME : 30

    SUMMER LAMENT : 31

    LAMENT : 32

TRIGGER WARNING: THE FAMILY HELIX : 33

    PSYCHOSIS : 34

    HEAD DOWN : 35

    HOMELESS. THREE KIDS. GOD BLESS : 36

    DEATH TO PRONOUNS : 38

    AN ATTEMPT : 40

    SACRIFICE : 41

    ALEXA : 42

    THE GRIEVING SEASON : 43

    MY COUSINS : 44

TRIGGER WARNING: GRAPHIC SKIN : 45
    WEDDED TO A SEX ADDICT (RAPIST) : 46
    PAVING : 49
    BLACKBIRD MARRIAGE : 50
    SELF PORTRAIT : 52
    MOST IMPORTANT : 54
    WILD WORDS : 55
    AFTER : 56
    ANATOMY LESSON : 57
    APRIL 21, 2011 : 58
    ANGER : 60
    THRESHOLDS : 61
    POST TRAUMATIC STRESS : 62
    ASSUMPTION : 64
    COUP D' ETAT : 65
    I WILL NEVER FORGIVE : 66
    SURGEON GENERAL'S WARNING : 67
    RETURN TO SENDER : 68

A RENEWAL : 69
    WHEN THE MOON IS STRONG : 71
    BREATHTAKING SCENE : 72
    EVAPORATION : 73
    UNTITLED : 74
    MEDITATION : 77

A Beginning

Sunset Story

taking a long time, arrive
test your legs
tip your head and your neck, spine
out of your shoulders the story of this summer night

not yet open, the cover is heavy
with the sunset peeling day away
lilting pink and lavender
then long shadows walk in the canyon dust like fables
coyote, eagle, snake
a wink of planet pins the sky
like a cactus prick blooming pain
which is natural and right
what of the tale comforts us
like a grandmother pat on your hand

become pine sap from a new campfire spark
send a wail to the air
of what is low and sorrowed
bone deep arrive to this circle, this fire ring
bring all sights and senses
we are attentive and watchful – not sleeping now

1.

I travel alone
take breakfast
hard and slam down
book with a slapface
don't care if it's a ways
from your place
because I'll walk there anyway
whole without your shoes
beside me. It doesn't matter much
because I don't speak in sentences
only a clip of a line from a song
it crows out from me – not from my
mouth but from my ribs or darker sides
I sling my bag of wreckage high
but not fast enough, so top arch
it pours and falls on my head
to disperse on the sidewalk
but I've already moved along
and I still travel alone

2.

infinite worlds of microscopic dust particles built upside down
the desire of each hair along the shin or forearm
to blow northward in shadows
of solitude or togetherness
or south-lean hunger grass and leaf with digging claws
What pain stabs you there middle minded and scowling
at the floor tiles?

3.

flow will come between
the sea and sadness
find a den under brambles
and behind granite boulders
with a thick paper cut cheek
and razor skinned finger
open your teeth and jaw
hinges oddly angled,
rock, just crumble history and resolve
to defeat your smallness
with growing nerve
along your sideways
headache
ramble over all other sound
even some laughter and talk
your words scrumble into their
minds and pick-ax stick that
stone or slate
running water over rapidly
and beyond just life and reverse
until nothing light opens in the
morning

4.

"Even the word speaks of water."
    — Julia Cameron, *The Sound of Paper*

Give up the writing way of this in the lines
and against the grain of the book.
Write until my fingers are blistered,
row until my shoulders give out.

Rake me, hold me.
Chains drive us to the hollow places of might.
Let go the shelter,
run out into the wildness
and the yellow of midnight is dull and painful.

bend now forward to hang from your waist
kneel now
like a pair of pants that don't fit
and shoes that flit and flip
nearly stumbling this one Sunday

where so much rain makes the flower
beds choke with weeds
stir the earth, stir to mud

insignificant insects curl in the air
like ash and spark from the fire
the fire is loaded

but blues

even the word speaks of water
never drink from the rivers
they run brown and laden with running dirt

Dance of Ashes

Today, a hovering edge in time:
cold dust
falls past our fingers,
pulling the air tighter
drunkenly, as if it would warm us.

We prowl angry in our skin.
Our bones are crumbling
structures in the dance of ashes.

An absence of scent:
acidic breath erodes walls
twisted shards pressed into the tile
wires melted in metallic pools
snowflakes thunder
in this quiet
heavy in this fragmented darkness
We are stapled into existence
without permission
dust collects in our mouths,
which we opened to complain.

This is our mark in an entangled age.

"To write," Marguerite Duras remarked, "is also not to speak. It is to keep silent. It is to howl noiselessly."

—Terry Tempest Williams

Hot Spell

Aggressively restless on this day
try to wear less and less
and the swelter sticks
despite the rough washcloth dipped in cool water
grumble loudly to strangers
how we hate the sweat of noon
even a cool glass of tea
drips on the outside and weakens with the ice melt
our tongues swell
we barely move
except our lids blink with salty stinging
this summer
even a pinch too much
even to provoke

so climb into this heat
roll it over your cheeks
and drip down your neck
between your breasts
and the back of your knees
it's not alluring
it crawls along your curves
and spiders on your back
you can't wear a hat for shade
even birdsong is tired
languish here, your glasses slide forward
off your nose, but you don't care
in this heavy humid
and groggy numberless day

Trigger Warning:
Blood and Bone

What comes?
    when we buckle our knees and go quiet
    stepping into footprints larger than our own feet
    graves where our people are buried
    and cradles for new babes
What comes?
    when we think of eyes in so many colors
    when all skin feels soft but cracking and wrinkling
    under power of gravity and levity
What comes?
    to the particles of sand and microbes of ocean
    where all the solids are just tighter and tighter compression
What comes?
    depression when never enough
    or too much crushes us
    one mass at a time
    without strength for resisting
What comes? What comes?
    something bigger than ourselves
    how many more is eight billion?
    and sixteen billion shoes

Terror Today

Fragile the heart's high alert
pounding
like the pistol hammer falling
pounding
like the gun powder explosions
with each trigger pull.

split second choice
flee or freeze
climb over rows of laminated desks
or hide in the shadows
beneath

the shoes left behind
backpacks and books left behind
because all that matters is
to live.

ellipses crack across the back of the lecture hall
fragile is the small empty hole –
puncturing the desktop
only as wide as a pen, really

fragile the student
dying
clutching an uncapped
highlighter

fragile the first responder
hands holding another student's
head together.

fragile the emergency radio channel chatter
requesting more, help
and the fog descends like a first aid
blanket unfolding in the fragile air

and with us weakened
it comes again…
it comes again…

"Color is all. When color is right, form is right. Color is everything, color is vibration like music; everything is vibration."
—Marc Chagall, Artist, *America Windows*

Independence Day: PFLAG Dirge
for the Orlando Pulse Victims

Street music this July afternoon

    blood-blue shapes

shine and mingle,

      people waited for the parade

      for us, a funeral procession.

Glow against the looker-skin

    shifting weight over then over.

Our colors reflect all colors:

    we walk for those forbidden from home,

glass-delicate and strong.

This lead-plate fragility,

    for lost sons and daughters,

these pane-captured honest shapes

    and found humans who sparkle best in the daylight

walking songs. Clear art swoops around,
        but a guy gave me the finger:
floating sun-high and branch-graceful.
        I blew him a kiss.
Rose bloom in the corner, left.

Our sight-eyes gleam for the
        kisses for mothers and fathers
they rose as we walked.

Building windows, higher
        quietly stirred— they applauded
hopes, and winds blow low,
        some alone
we were hushed and loud
        we were strong.

And we walked by
        for the people of Pulse and our own,
beneath the politic breath
        of rainbow streamers, dove wings,
and waving American flags.

Curving Away*

when we, America
round on ourselves – curve away
you are not my country

a person makes a love
and they hold each other
timed against the next bombing or gunner

I taste gunpowder news with my coffee.

someone kills children sleeping
or kills them awake
blowing them out of their shoes
or were they just feet?

Only our skeletons, the same.
No race to ligaments.
No religion to tendons.

Trim your nails,
clip your pain at the root.
cover me
cover you

But this tile, this carpet
these flicker lights
give nowhere to hide.

Do we lay down?
Do we charge?

Cry out to the powerful.
Hang your head in the new quiet.
Resounding in the night.

Echoed east or west
until nobody is left.

*Title taken from the line "curving away from the story"
from "Stones (The Coast of Turkey, Robert Smithson)"
by Ann Lauterbach

Shock and Awe

Somehow on a certain day
        an anniversary of the deaths of five students in class

we look back in surprise now
        because it is not horrific enough to be mentioned

I heard from someone that survived
he paused in the mayhem
enjoying chaos and death's breath in February

        he shook his head slowly—not enough

        and then reloaded

Strange Steve—they wrote a book about him and conjectured
what someday did he daydream about
with a cruel smile

to make us wonder what sort of crazy enough
stalked the auditorium

and then, on stage, where I also had attended class
in the auditorium almost twenty some years ago
the end
like a terrible tragedy

he bit the shotgun barrel
        and we found the slug in the projector screen

after sometime had passed

Some years later again
      we cry together, holding photos and lighting candles

For Orlando, Aurora, Sandy Hook, Paris

cell phones ring the death toll
death echoes in the institutions

and I read someone's comment

the only thing that saves us daily, nightly
in every part of our dependency
      is that no one came here
                      to kill today

For Next Time

when blood flows on the street or in buildings
when death-cruel fear holds us
and people go running out, away in any way

we fold up when grazed by violence like venus fly traps
we gather each other under blankets
arms to chest for quiet
our ears to chest for proof of beating

gather with candles to slow sing
to lay to rest

what else can we do but wake?
we are only cell and bone and hair

when we gather we are softer

Summer Lament

June white peonies bang open
like flour sacks spilling petals
dipped low from heavy fullness
catch them in the thumb-index web

of your hand
and send them swinging
like hanging bodies

though they protest and we black ants
fall to the ground
racing on unconcerned or scared

and we stand still at 1,040 mph
in crowds or alone
here or there

pop-pop of frustration of hate
bullets end worlds
the garden razed
bombs rend skin from bone
and blood from muscle

a horror in place and time

but the maples still run sap
drip again
and the crab apples fruit

Lament (After Rumi)

Find the shining people
touched by grief and transformed

Rumi says "a wealth you cannot imagine flows through you."

For every terrorist there are a thousand painters, poets
but there are not as many healers as bomb particles or bullets

Is there love for every hate?
      A petal for every tear?

Words are neutral until perceived.
      But do we all sing?
      Don't you bleed?

Trigger Warning:
The Family Helix

Psychosis

Come out, God.

blood, violence, cages
stuck and the addict
doesn't sleep

the world slides sideways
lights and color

and a tear slides from my eye
with a secret locked
just freeze and hug your pillow tight
or swing—
careen through the night

on the road,
scared rabbit, run on.

Head Down

head down,
bowing walk along the traffic lanes
tattered sign
splitting plastic overstuffed bags
unfold in the city
spilling guts on the curb
and motorists drive over the roadkill

hot wavy emissions choke the air, paid for
in blood or money

water, pray
give water, small
a bottle
cold relief
press to neck and brow

given a place on the median
shuffle by
shuffle by

Homeless. Three kids. God Bless.

Man, you are a star particle light seed
of life and beauty, but these heart faces
with blind eyes pass you on the side street,
give you no second glance.

You label yourself down on your luck,
layered and it's high time for the promise
of forgiveness but they are cursing loudly
instead at the traffic light hold up. Here's my
tiny white blanket now to cover your steady
styled loss, with the driven
snow and wind howl today.

You bless me and I bless you more.
This is how we conform to just dust, our basic level
make-up. I'm awake now and I hear how
your blood rushes to flush your skin, especially
for the painful welts and where your swollen hands
give you away. And your downcast humble
humanity expects nothing more than recognition
of your poor circumstance.

I see you. I ask your name and where you are from,
it feels so inadequate in comparison to a meal
or a place for you to go. I slip you a twenty
and see your stiff garments that have had no
washing and no safe place to dry out.

Jason, I'll tell the story of our brief
meeting. How your brown eyes
caught me close with near tears. I glance at you,
now in the rear view mirror, glimmering
with a sadness, but another driver stops to pass you a
heavy weighted shopping bag. One at a time
we do our best to see you through. We pray it's enough.

Death to Pronouns

August heat. My child tried to die.
She took a bottleful of pills to sleep forever, but I found him.
It's so hot. But hospital blankets: fleece or cotton?
Blue or pink stocking hat?
When we found her. When I found him.

Little girl, we had hoped to dress
you for prom and braid your hair,
we tried to make you cut
papery hearts and glue glitter surprises.
Maybe someday she'll even ring
her finger like little chime bells
and blush powder will dust the sinktop.

Instead, you relished lining up
plastic animals in epic battles on the rug
and they fought
bloody soaking
wrenching wars. Slashing violence of claw and tooth.

My Hes and Shes—so jumbled together, but
they are as distinctly separate
as His and Hers public restrooms.
Or shoes. Heels or wingtips?

Warmer. Warmer, but this was no hide-and-seek.
It's life or death.

I found him. And her pulse had cooled.
When I found her
she wouldn't wake up and
I drove to the ER, feeling long ago
birthpains.

Close sweaty, hot smelly summer night. She did not die.
But he was born.

I watch his posture—now,
he's walking manlike.
His voice, deep.
His chin angles
strong and hard.

Laugh mighty big and lumber. Come, let me look closer.

There is no great change here.
Only an establishment of truth.
Like storm-front cold
wind flushing the medicines and blowing freedom.

I love your form and soul and self, my boy.
I found you. Now we live.

An Attempt

When you find an empty pill bottle
and he wants to die,
catch yourself rocking
to the rhythm of your grown child's anguish.
Your toes grip the carpet
so you don't fall apart.
You cradle him
into the stretcher
and try to hold his hand to cross the street.

Sacrifice

wild palpitations
of a ripped open pomegranate
I hear the release song
as it drips freshly
through my fingers, alive
juicy stains hum the webbed
roads of my skin to break and burst
the kernels against my violent teeth
praise for the sweet licking heart
the seed of God and death resolving
into life and ever breaking
mourning, brings death again.

Alexa (after Sylvia Plath)

Sigh please sigh, sigh please sigh
      while you stand nearby.
It's hard being scared
of teeth in the night
and my throat dares to dry.

I heard your cry. A life in one moment
velvet-breathing, my body
and you quite serene,
one eyelash small
like a moth wing.

Your weight settled slightly
like an October light over the fields-
a haven of purplish waves.
A harvest caught with blades
and they cut, cut, cut.

You do not speak or lie.
I'm too scared to reply.
I'd choke on the words and my tongue
has caught on the fence.
A silent voice and a voiceless silence.

The wind off the fields, the smell of that air
is the closest thought nearby.
Your sweet Irish component,
and a stone to kiss, and a stone to kiss
Little fingerprint, your tender thighs.
I've a pain in my side and with your tears,
scarred child, I cry.

The Grieving Season

February screams out
each moment
aches slow

shots fired and car crash

And I'm sobbing to God.

I slide over to the passenger seat
I confess my secret heart
Shaped darkness sloped and angry
with broken glass, torn metal

each precious life's cells
gasping lastly

each grieving season I hold
my breath remembering each
of you lost

My thoughts jump and crackle
breaking me fully open
little ambush

My Cousins

Their deaths come full on
like a car crash.
October is not the dying season.
Instead February leans in to the frozen middle
solid and rends open,
twisting the pain more. Like how you can
break a sapling and spin the bark around
it just twines tighter and suffocates more
with icicles and frost breath.
Air too frigid to stink, but death hangs
near on naked tree limbs taking my good people.
But where is your good comfort, God?

The list of them goes on forever
like the wisps of ice feathers
on the frozen sidewalk.
Tread lightly here.
I loved them.

Trigger Warning:
Graphic Skin

Wedded to a Sex Addict (Rapist)

On a couple's most sacred night,
secret rib and dusky thigh,
you bruised me—
in the limo
on the way to the reception.

You hiked the white dress slip up around my waist
and my eyes pleaded out the window
over your shoulder.

I saw your brother
as he waited for the light to change,
but the windows were tinted
and you plunged ahead.

Later, in my flower-wreath crown
lit in the hotel lamplight
you took my picture, veiled
as you gagged me, blithely
with my thumbprint petal cheek tear.

In my shift eye
I try to think that nothing much
happened there.

I scrubbed myself to shower you off
in the morning, but
you came 'round again
with your camera, caught
me on film,
and no one saw those wedding photos.

Except the ones you posted
on the XXX website
with me in the lamplight
from the hotel.

Now, what do I say to my
youngself?

Oh honey—
that ain't no moon.

"And it's been here silent all these years."
—Tori Amos

Paving

So the day spins and yawns lately
opening like a leaf, unfurling
as a woman who takes off her coat
then suit jacket in the hall after rain
I am laying in gray green cement
pulled up to my chin
secured there strongly with rebar bones
I don't yell out or dig frantic
but as I stay I feel a heavy panic
to at least swipe my hair away
from my face, it's plastered to my lips
with an unmoving cheek
and a closing off of sense

What happened to this day?
Now I move, I flex brittle
breaking up in heavy pieces
somehow I must walk again.

Blackbird Marriage

Each step you take toward me
carpet crunches as loud as gravel, heavy
nowhere to flee—
take flight
so the blackbird sings through the night.

Silent voice down the hall
against the wall
(against the wall).

Rough, the sheet on my cheek
when you push me on my face.
Your belt buckle clangs
like a church bell and
I pray to God for protection and
deliverance from evil.

Sing myself a lavender lullaby
Let slumber fill your eyes
and try to smile when you rise.

Shadows down the hall
against the wall
(against the wall).

Yanking my clothes up and down
like venetian blinds
tearing me apart; open and shut.
Take broken wings and try to fly.
Flutter of wings down the hall
against the wall
(against the wall).

Purple my raw eyelids
after wiping too many tears; awake now.
Murmurs are my screams
no one hears.
Purple, the sour bruises;
blackberry stains no one sees.

Blackbird, fly—take flight
pray the broken blackbird lives through the night.

Self Portrait

sometimes hide in the back of the closet
with the leather and gun oil smell
crying with the force of a million women
without voices or too loud laughing
crazy eyes flicker from watchfulness

why, this bruise blooms on my upper arm
shapely oval prints
first pink, then blue purple
then aging green-yellow stains
or this time teeth marks
on the bridge of my nose
and me writhing

how, I clasp my knees tightly
while he peels my strength away
like saplings, he rends
I can't cover enough
I can't hold enough
I yield because fighting
makes it worse

why, struggle when you always lose?

my mind scene clear
I pull the ceiling closer—
counting the pixel points
of how many ceilings?

Is this room plum color and vanilla,
like the skin of my thigh
on days like this?

Hours after,
I'm weak like the dregs of tea
I pour it out as dribbles
on the bathroom tile.

"A poem can begin with a lie"
—Adrienne Rich, *Cartographies of Silence 1*

Most Important

A woman stares long at the table.
      She is fine.
French toast stales on the plate.
      It is good.
Forget what happened.
      Never did.

The poet can begin with a lie and a truth.
I don't want to cry out.
I choke on words.

What is not written
is the most important.

Wild Words

language of pace and plums
speaks and whispers of secrets
carry them in a canvas bag
slap me on the thighs for attention
I can't bear it
blow your hair dry
make up your eyes
with attention to the lashes and lips
praying "Mary"

but curse and lie your way out of there
sailing on a river of blues mowing down greens
keep the blossoms
but the only thing to do next is ask why
I think she could help

After

I prefer to burn my skin
beneath the scathing shower.
Blast the memory of touch
and steam-bleach my thoughts.
I shave the cells away blankly with care
grooming is clean and good
but ineffective. Haunting
men have stood over me soiling
what I wish was mine alone.
So scrape without cutting
is the best I can do now.

Anatomy Lesson

I wear apologies in my eyes daily.
And I draw red loneliness on my lips,
      to tell you the truth about my mouth.
I have scolded my hands for writing again.
And the grief of my spine slumps, exhausted.

I can't raise my head because I'm closing
      off words in my throat.
I shift in my seat and hold my sweater—
      small comfort, like a blanket.

But don't mistake me for weak or easy.
Or I'll strike you with my knee—
      for I won't stand to call myself
      broken much longer.

April 21, 2011

I'm not talking about the kind of running
people do to stay in shape.
It's fight or flight – *baby, I'm sorry.*

I won't do it again.

It's the run you do after twelve years'
marriage when you realize you
will die unless you
pack only to survive,
take your children out of school,
and drive.

Because when the risk weighs
heavy and chokes your words, steady
now. You just must put one foot in front
of the other, mechanically.

Lift your foot, bend your knee, lower now.
You can't run, I'll find you

and lift, bend your knee, lower
I'll hunt you down

lift faster,
bend knee

(—*slap*—)
remember?

So lift before he gets home.
Hurry, bend your knees
flee
one foot in front
of the other—

toe the line
of live or die.

Anger

I don't know how to wear my anger.
Do I fashion it into a soft neck scarf
worn to cover the fingerprint bruise
he left under my right side jaw?

Should I button sleeves over my wrists
he held them above my head?

The blue blood ways are a roadmap
of every opportunity to resist not taken.

I feel the robe rage
with a sash around my middle.
The thick terry cloth binding
and he pinned me
beneath him with just one
forearm across my breast-bone.

How do I wear my screams
my voice whisper-thin
but my walking grief unstoppable?

But sit there in your discomfort.
Yes. Right there.
Let's see how brave you are.

Thresholds

All I can think of is this house
and blue flower petals
after burned by the sun, evolving
a named oil painting
or stained glass window pane
I'm shackled to walls
in this big house
of our marriage
which I blew away
like dust on the mantel
I drag the slipcovers
across the hardwood
draping, draping
they cascade down the stairs
like seas and hard impact
like the biggest wave
when I take the last step of ever
I escape the chains of your bloodlust
I render in poetry
the clash of me saving my life
against your blocking me
in the courtroom
those pews, that corner
the house made me smaller
always smaller

Post Traumatic Stress

1.

Eleven watercolor birds
strung together with teal ribbon
twist in my still bedroom
not quite above my pillow

I wake some terror-soaked nights
and counting my pulse down
I imagine they fly from the window
in all directions.

2.

I don't want to write the darkness

I loosen the pain like a collar
I wish these tights on my legs grip
so that you can't get them off

you see-sawed your way into me
and I am haunted

let the children sleep
pray they don't hear you topping me

do you know what it's like to come out of your body?

I go to the place and lie in the mountain stream
and everything that happens in reverse

first I am raped
and then unraped, untouched
and only then I smile

3.

I chase in the chase of my dreams
sleep in the no sleep restlessness
like shaming

there is no exhausted restful place for me
I rub my eyes wider

put on your shoes
flashlight, we go in

scratch my arms with needlepoint
paint my skin with leaves

tumult like choking angry venom
wasp sting across my thighs

Assumption

Red suede five-inch platform heels
take me for a walk
a little blonder

and he said

"you have red shoes"
with a knowing smile.

Coup d'état

I paced my walk today
along the wood's edge,
prowled,
furious at the maples—
ungroomed and their cowlick branches
stuck in-the-air salute,
but they are not all I know of betrayal.

So my ex-husband wants to battle
over my dead body

Righteously I marched towards
the breaking creek
and hauled a stone *three times his fist-size*
dragged the past out
to line it up on the bridge rail
for a pass and review.

I named it by his last name
and heaved the plunker
into silt water depths.

He only plunges to the bottom,
imagine his bound hands no struggle
I don't pray over him.

There can only be one leader here—
and this is my revolution.

I Will Never Forgive

What does your apology sound like
in this distilled and distasteful silence?

Hum from your distant lips—words,
words to take the sad promise of my eyes
and fit them instead with hope.

The drumming of choppy regret by your tongue
pleases me simply because of your discomfort.
You wait for me to release your uncertainty
— but I won't.

Crash your teeth together, with those lost for nothing phrases.
Push your sorrys out and away from your mouth—
swing them left and right because I'm not over and done.
Flap your cheeks, blow and whine,
call, call on me to relieve your anguish
but I still won't forgive you.

Even if your apology sounds low and sincere
a purr to my ear and you crawl on a humble-to-the-knees grief
I still remember the slicing and sliding of you

Surgeon General's Warning

I want to be a cigarette writer.
Each inhale my words burn you
and exhale – pollute you with a
smoky second-hand punch-in-the-nose.
Punch in your face.
I hope you'll read my books that
behind-the-garage-with-a-couple-of-matches
spark day. And you'll find out
these dragon-flaming
camel-spitting poems
leave their nicotine stain.

Hide your porn mags on the outside
but, cheater like, read me inside
because neither of us will ever forget

and I want to cancer you back.

Return to Sender

This is what happens
when you break and run for your life
the mail tries to catch you up

But
that's not my name anymore
I cut my hair off
and I'm in the garden now

I bake pies and paint in color
I can sleep now
and my new love

Kisses me on the forehead.

A Renewal

"Now something so sad has hold of us that the breath leaves and we can't even cry."

—Charles Bukowski

When the Moon Is Strong

When the moon is strong
blood flows in all directions.

There is enough for pause.
    I will not mother again.
    From the wing flutter of the first quickening
    to the hard clench of contraction,
    when I bathed and scooped warm water
    across my rounded middle
    and each flex of you
    was a stretch of me.
But never again.
Surely my time is growing short.
Ask me for another.
I can see the new skin glow now.
A little whisper-suck at my breast.
Reaching across the darkened sky
when the moon is strong.

Breathtaking Scene

Come behind me no words between us
it is enough to scent you this stillness.
Always reach for my shoulders—
twist my head around
with a graze of your finger.
I'll close my sad eyes
revel in this never-touching chaos
near you flying ribbons from my wrists like kites
to your throat soft part
at my lips there swallow more, try to taste me
like you did
in this dizzy nearness
this fate pulling rose-aroused and bright
high never spoken aloud
just dance unpaired, sway alone
in the light spun night.

Evaporation

beside your face
and not touching
to feel the swoon of the air
I search in your eyes for
the daily face of yours: creased irritation and bitterness
or madness
a madness of my own
when you lit up, when you finally saw me
you took my face in your hands
I closed my eyes
how you sound
when I risked to look again
there was no you there
I run my hands along the cushion
searching for a hint, some remaining warmth
some of my name in your eyes
but now I'm not sure you knew me
after all

1.

"If [I] could simply look you in the face."
                      —Adrienne Rich, *Cartographies of Silence 7*

keeper of my skins togetherness
gatherer of the leaking tears
sayer of all glorious words of love
if I could simply look you in the face
in first morning light
I will be motionless, not rising
still as stone pavers walked barefoot
I could watch your chest rise and fall
ocean waves; tide surfing with the sea sheets
and ripple quilt-foaming
while I watch, songs will pass in my mind
I will mouth them infantly
turning the lyric over again
borrowing the best word to write your poem later
toucher of my body
tracer of my rounded lines
giver of sleep or bare waking
I study your hair
curling in the heat sweat of night between us
thin lids, ribboned in blue
your warm blood beneath

2.

It only rains when we are together.
Every love we leave from your torrent.
dew on the clover
puddle in the easement

creeks from your mouth
rivers from between our legs
great lakes surround us lying here
seas of bed and touch-skin oceans
rise, fall
tide, pull back
shower our heads
soak for our bodies
pool together
tear apart

3.

Pass this way just once again
like an old road or fruit tree
I crave your step of quickened
life laugh crazy pain
because I saw you walking
hurried home late afternoon
spring sun setting in your eyes
but I know you felt my going
by in the swooping held notes
of the car horn
I would shadow behind you and
cover your eyes and wishfully you
would smile and turn around
You took nothing away but the moment
your hands as empty as your stride

"to love life, to love it even
when you have no stomach for it and everything you've held dear
crumbles like burnt paper in your hands
...you think, How can a body
withstand this?
Then you hold life like a face between your palms, a plain face,
no charming smile, no violet eyes
and you say, yes, I will take you."

—Ellen Bass

Meditation

Sometimes
we struggle with our private phantoms
and sometimes in the savage silence
we touch, our shadows blend,
and we decide on creation.

A soap bubble bends
trembling slightly
under the weight of the universe.

Jen May is a poet warrior. As a former police officer, she has witnessed much grief and inhumanity. As a writer, she refuses to give up hope.

Jen May is a founding member of Open Sky Poets in the Fox Valley, Illinois region. You may have seen her read at an open mic at A-Town Poetics or Harmonious Howl. She has been a featured reader at Waterline Writers, Lit by the Bridge, and Mutual Ground's Survivor's Art Show. Jen has previously served as editor of two fine arts magazines, *Byzantium* and *Towers*. Most recently, she has been published in the *Journal of Modern Poetry 19: Poetry of Protest*.

Visit her blog www.JenMayPoems.com for posts on the arts, charity, compassionate humanism, words, writing prompts, and poetic form. May is working on her next book, *Midnight Birdsong*.

An excerpt from the forthcoming:
Midnight Birdsong

Roots

Plant on Good Friday.

Harvest in change months.

Find the clod mass of starch-meat:

potato, rutabaga, carrot.

Trim the root hairs.

Try to skin away now, peel—

dig out the scars and eyes.

Scrub them fresh.

Make stew. Pair with wine.

Pepper with warming

spices and herbs.

Taste with a gentle spoon.

Dip your crust of bread now.

If too hot, await its cooling.

But save some in your root bin—

cellar straw preserved.

Quarter them and hoe them in piles.

Plant on Good Friday.

Harvest in change months.

www.ingramcontent.com/pod-product-compliance
Lightning Source LLC
Chambersburg PA
CBHW070758050426
42452CB00012B/2392